Baby, You're Here!

BABY,
you're here!

A One-Line-a-Day
BABY MEMORY BOOK

BY CRYSTAL REAGAN

ROCKRIDGE
PRESS

Interior and Cover Designer: Lisa Forde

Art Producer: Janice Ackerman

Editor: Orli Zuravicky

Production Editor: Andrew Yackira

Illustrations: © Shutterstock

ISBN: Print 978-1-64152-810-8

This memory book *is all about*

_____.

"The best and most beautiful things in the world cannot be seen or even touched—they must be felt with the heart."

— HELEN KELLER

Baby, You're Here!

Welcoming a new baby into the world is a time full of excitement and anticipation. Every parent longs to hear those three little words that give their life such deep meaning: **Baby, you're here!** This new person in charge is under two feet tall, doesn't weigh much more than a sack of potatoes, and yells out orders in a language you don't understand. But the time you spend together will create a lifetime of memories that will overflow from the pages of this memory journal.

Your baby will grow and change at an astonishing rate. Begin your memory journey by capturing important details about your newborn here:

Full Name: _____

Due Date: _____

Birth Date: _____

Birth Time: _____

Birthplace: _____

Weight: _____

Length: _____

Hair Color: _____

Eye Color: _____

Blood Type: _____

"You can learn many things from children. How much patience you have, for instance."

 — FRANKLIN P. JONES

A Year with You

The next twelve months will be a magical time full of bonding with baby as you experience the wonder of being a family together. Use this section to record your thoughts and day-to-day feelings and discoveries about your new little one. The first year goes by so quickly—capture what being a parent is like and how baby is changing your life on the pages of this journal so you'll never forget these first days, weeks, and months. There is room for journaling daily memories week by week, and for recording monthly milestones like baby's first crawl, first words, first steps, first haircut, and more. Write the story of your baby's first year, and create a keepsake you will cherish forever.

Your First Week

On the day you came, the weather was _____

_____.

The biggest news of the day was _____

_____

_____.

MONDAY ___ / ___ / ___

_____

_____

_____

_____

_____

4

TUESDAY ___ / ___ / ___

_____

_____

_____

_____

WEDNESDAY ___ / ___ / ___

_____

_____

_____

_____

THURSDAY ___ / ___ / ___

_____

_____

_____

_____

_____

FRIDAY ___ / ___ / ___

_____

_____

_____

_____

SATURDAY ___ / ___ / ___

_____

_____

_____

_____

SUNDAY ___ / ___ / ___

_____

_____

_____

_____

_____

Your Second Week

The very first time I saw you, I felt _____

_____

_____

_____

_____ .

MONDAY ___ / ___ / ___

_____

_____

_____

_____

_____

TUESDAY ___ / ___ / ___

_____

_____

_____

_____

WEDNESDAY ___ / ___ / ___

_____

_____

_____

_____

THURSDAY ___ / ___ / ___

_____

_____

_____

_____

FRIDAY ___ / ___ / ___

_____

_____

_____

_____

_____

SATURDAY ___ / ___ / ___

_____

_____

_____

_____

SUNDAY ___ / ___ / ___

_____

_____

_____

_____

Your Third Week

Everyone was excited to meet you. Your first visitor was _____

_____

_____

_____

_____ .

MONDAY ___ / ___ / ___

_____

_____

_____

_____

TUESDAY ___ / ___ / ___

_____

_____

_____

_____

_____

WEDNESDAY ___ / ___ / ___

_____

_____

_____

_____

THURSDAY ___ / ___ / ___

_____

_____

_____

_____

FRIDAY ___ / ___ / ___

_____

_____

_____

_____

SATURDAY ___ / ___ / ___

_____

_____

_____

_____

SUNDAY ___ / ___ / ___

_____

_____

_____

_____

Your Fourth Week

You hate it when _____
_____
_____
_____
_____.

_____
_____
_____
_____
_____

TUESDAY ___ / ___ / ___

_____
_____
_____
_____

WEDNESDAY ___ / ___ / ___

_____
_____
_____
_____

THURSDAY ___ / ___ / ___

_____
_____
_____
_____

FRIDAY ___ / ___ / ___

_____

_____

_____

_____

_____

SATURDAY ___ / ___ / ___

_____

_____

_____

_____

SUNDAY ___ / ___ / ___

_____

_____

_____

_____

Your Fifth Week

You outgrew your newborn clothing at _____

_____

_____

_____

_____.

MONDAY ___ / ___ / ___

_____

_____

_____

_____

_____

TUESDAY ___ / ___ / ___

_____

_____

_____

_____

_____

WEDNESDAY ___ / ___ / ___

_____

_____

_____

_____

THURSDAY ___ / ___ / ___

_____

_____

_____

_____

FRIDAY ___ / ___ / ___

_____

_____

_____

_____

_____

SATURDAY ___ / ___ / ___

_____

_____

_____

_____

SUNDAY ___ / ___ / ___

_____

_____

_____

_____

Your Sixth Week

The best way to soothe you when you're upset is _____

_____

_____

_____

_____ .

MONDAY ____ / ____ / ____

_____

_____

_____

_____

_____

TUESDAY ___ / ___ / ___

_____

_____

_____

_____

WEDNESDAY ___ / ___ / ___

_____

_____

_____

_____

THURSDAY ___ / ___ / ___

_____

_____

_____

_____

FRIDAY ___ / ___ / ___

_____

_____

_____

_____

SATURDAY ___ / ___ / ___

_____

_____

_____

_____

SUNDAY ___ / ___ / ___

_____

_____

_____

_____

Your Seventh Week

During our first few weeks together, the funniest thing that

happened was _____

_____

_____

_____ .

MONDAY ___ / ___ / ___

_____

_____

_____

_____

_____

TUESDAY ___ / ___ / ___

_____

_____

_____

_____

WEDNESDAY ___ / ___ / ___

_____

_____

_____

_____

THURSDAY ___ / ___ / ___

_____

_____

_____

_____

_____

FRIDAY ___ / ___ / ___

_____
_____
_____
_____

SATURDAY ___ / ___ / ___

_____
_____
_____
_____

SUNDAY ___ / ___ / ___

_____
_____
_____
_____
_____

Your Eighth Week

You love seeing the world around you. The first thing your eyes
focused on was _____

_____

_____

_____.

MONDAY ___ / ___ / ___

_____

_____

_____

_____

_____

TUESDAY ___ / ___ / ___

_____

_____

_____

_____

WEDNESDAY ___ / ___ / ___

_____

_____

_____

_____

THURSDAY ___ / ___ / ___

_____

_____

_____

_____

_____

FRIDAY ___ / ___ / ___

_____
_____
_____
_____

SATURDAY ___ / ___ / ___

_____
_____
_____
_____

SUNDAY ___ / ___ / ___

_____
_____
_____
_____
_____

Your Ninth Week

The first time you smiled, you were smiling at _____

_____

_____

_____

_____.

MONDAY ___ / ___ / ___

_____

_____

_____

_____

TUESDAY ___ / ___ / ___

_____

_____

_____

_____

WEDNESDAY ___ / ___ / ___

_____

_____

_____

_____

THURSDAY ___ / ___ / ___

_____

_____

_____

_____

FRIDAY ___ / ___ / ___

_____

_____

_____

_____

SATURDAY ___ / ___ / ___

_____

_____

_____

_____

SUNDAY ___ / ___ / ___

_____

_____

_____

_____

Your Tenth Week

Your first coo was in response to _____

_____

_____

_____

_____.

_____

_____

_____

_____

_____

TUESDAY ___ / ___ / ___

_____

_____

_____

_____

WEDNESDAY ___ / ___ / ___

_____

_____

_____

_____

THURSDAY ___ / ___ / ___

_____

_____

_____

_____

FRIDAY ___ / ___ / ___

_____

_____

_____

_____

_____

SATURDAY ___ / ___ / ___

_____

_____

_____

_____

SUNDAY ___ / ___ / ___

_____

_____

_____

_____

Your Eleventh
Week

My desire for your future is that you _____

_____

_____.

MONDAY ___ / ___ / ___

_____

_____

_____

_____

_____

TUESDAY ___ / ___ / ___

_____

_____

_____

_____

WEDNESDAY ___ / ___ / ___

_____

_____

_____

_____

THURSDAY ___ / ___ / ___

_____

_____

_____

_____

_____

FRIDAY ___ / ___ / ___

_____

_____

_____

_____

SATURDAY ___ / ___ / ___

_____

_____

_____

_____

SUNDAY ___ / ___ / ___

_____

_____

_____

_____

_____

Your Twelfth Week

When you wake up from a nap, the first thing you like to do is

_____

_____

_____

_____.

MONDAY ____ / ____ / ____

_____

_____

_____

_____

_____

TUESDAY ___ / ___ / ___

_____

_____

_____

_____

WEDNESDAY ___ / ___ / ___

_____

_____

_____

_____

THURSDAY ___ / ___ / ___

_____

_____

_____

_____

_____

FRIDAY ___ / ___ / ___

_____

_____

_____

_____

SATURDAY ___ / ___ / ___

_____

_____

_____

_____

SUNDAY ___ / ___ / ___

_____

_____

_____

_____

_____

Your Thirteenth Week

Singing is good for the soul. You love it when I sing _____
_____
_____.

MONDAY ___ / ___ / ___

_____
_____
_____
_____
_____

TUESDAY ___ / ___ / ___

_____

_____

_____

_____

WEDNESDAY ___ / ___ / ___

_____

_____

_____

_____

THURSDAY ___ / ___ / ___

_____

_____

_____

_____

_____

FRIDAY ____ / ____ / ____

_____

_____

_____

_____

SATURDAY ____ / ____ / ____

_____

_____

_____

_____

SUNDAY ____ / ____ / ____

_____

_____

_____

_____

Your Fourteenth Week

Your favorite thing to do right before bedtime is _____

_____

_____.

MONDAY ___ / ___ / ___

_____

_____

_____

_____

_____

TUESDAY ___ / ___ / ___

_____

_____

_____

_____

WEDNESDAY ___ / ___ / ___

_____

_____

_____

_____

THURSDAY ___ / ___ / ___

_____

_____

_____

_____

_____

FRIDAY ___ / ___ / ___

_____

_____

_____

_____

SATURDAY ___ / ___ / ___

_____

_____

_____

_____

SUNDAY ___ / ___ / ___

_____

_____

_____

_____

_____

Your Fifteenth Week

The best advice I've received about parenting is _____

_____

_____.

MONDAY ___ / ___ / ___

_____

_____

_____

_____

_____

TUESDAY ___ / ___ / ___

_____

_____

_____

_____

WEDNESDAY ___ / ___ / ___

_____

_____

_____

_____

THURSDAY ___ / ___ / ___

_____

_____

_____

_____

_____

FRIDAY ___ / ___ / ___

_____

_____

_____

_____

SATURDAY ___ / ___ / ___

_____

_____

_____

_____

SUNDAY ___ / ___ / ___

_____

_____

_____

_____

_____

Your Sixteenth Week

The first time you reached out your arms for me, it made

me feel _____

_____.

MONDAY ___ / ___ / ___

_____

_____

_____

_____

_____

TUESDAY ___ / ___ / ___

_____

_____

_____

_____

WEDNESDAY ___ / ___ / ___

_____

_____

_____

_____

THURSDAY ___ / ___ / ___

_____

_____

_____

_____

_____

FRIDAY ____ / ____ / ____

_____

_____

_____

_____

SATURDAY ____ / ____ / ____

_____

_____

_____

_____

SUNDAY ____ / ____ / ____

_____

_____

_____

_____

_____

Your Seventeenth Week

You have changed my life in so many ways. The most
incredible is _____

_____.

MONDAY ____ / ____ / ____

_____

_____

_____

_____

_____

TUESDAY ___ / ___ / ___

_____
_____
_____
_____

WEDNESDAY ___ / ___ / ___

_____
_____
_____
_____

THURSDAY ___ / ___ / ___

_____
_____
_____
_____
_____

FRIDAY ___ / ___ / ___

_____

_____

_____

_____

SATURDAY ___ / ___ / ___

_____

_____

_____

_____

SUNDAY ___ / ___ / ___

_____

_____

_____

_____

Your Eighteenth Week

The address for the first place you called home was _____

_____

_____.

MONDAY ____ / ____ / ____

_____

_____

_____

_____

_____

TUESDAY ___ / ___ / ___

_____

_____

_____

_____

WEDNESDAY ___ / ___ / ___

_____

_____

_____

_____

THURSDAY ___ / ___ / ___

_____

_____

_____

_____

_____

FRIDAY ___ / ___ / ___

_____

_____

_____

_____

SATURDAY ___ / ___ / ___

_____

_____

_____

_____

SUNDAY ___ / ___ / ___

_____

_____

_____

_____

_____

Your Nineteenth Week

The first time you rolled over, you rolled over for _____
_____
_____.

MONDAY ___ / ___ / ___

_____
_____
_____
_____

TUESDAY ___ / ___ / ___

_____

_____

_____

_____

WEDNESDAY ___ / ___ / ___

_____

_____

_____

_____

THURSDAY ___ / ___ / ___

_____

_____

_____

_____

_____

FRIDAY ___ / ___ / ___

_____

_____

_____

_____

SATURDAY ___ / ___ / ___

_____

_____

_____

_____

SUNDAY ___ / ___ / ___

_____

_____

_____

_____

_____

Your Twentieth Week

You love it when I read to you. Your favorite book is _____

_____

_____.

MONDAY ___ / ___ / ___

_____

_____

_____

_____

_____

TUESDAY ___ / ___ / ___

_____

_____

_____

_____

WEDNESDAY ___ / ___ / ___

_____

_____

_____

_____

THURSDAY ___ / ___ / ___

_____

_____

_____

_____

_____

FRIDAY ___ / ___ / ___

_____

_____

_____

_____

SATURDAY ___ / ___ / ___

_____

_____

_____

_____

SUNDAY ___ / ___ / ___

_____

_____

_____

_____

_____

Your Twenty-First Week

You always laugh when I _____
_____
_____.

MONDAY ___ / ___ / ___

_____

_____

_____

_____

TUESDAY ___ / ___ / ___

_____

_____

_____

_____

WEDNESDAY ___ / ___ / ___

_____

_____

_____

_____

THURSDAY ___ / ___ / ___

_____

_____

_____

_____

_____

FRIDAY ___ / ___ / ___

_____

_____

_____

_____

SATURDAY ___ / ___ / ___

_____

_____

_____

_____

SUNDAY ___ / ___ / ___

_____

_____

_____

_____

_____

Your Twenty-Second Week

You're so perfect, you had to have the perfect name. The story behind your name is: _____

_____.

MONDAY ___ / ___ / ___

_____

_____

_____

_____

_____

TUESDAY ___ / ___ / ___

_____

_____

_____

_____

WEDNESDAY ___ / ___ / ___

_____

_____

_____

_____

THURSDAY ___ / ___ / ___

_____

_____

_____

_____

_____

FRIDAY ___ / ___ / ___

_____

_____

_____

_____

SATURDAY ___ / ___ / ___

_____

_____

_____

_____

SUNDAY ___ / ___ / ___

_____

_____

_____

_____

_____

Your Twenty-Third Week

Your favorite toy is _____
_____
_____.

MONDAY ___ / ___ / ___

_____
_____
_____
_____

TUESDAY ___ / ___ / ___

_____

_____

_____

_____

WEDNESDAY ___ / ___ / ___

_____

_____

_____

_____

THURSDAY ___ / ___ / ___

_____

_____

_____

_____

FRIDAY ___ / ___ / ___

_____

_____

_____

_____

SATURDAY ___ / ___ / ___

_____

_____

_____

_____

SUNDAY ___ / ___ / ___

_____

_____

_____

_____

_____

Your Twenty-Fourth Week

You love it when _____

_____

_____.

MONDAY ___ / ___ / ___

_____

_____

_____

_____

TUESDAY ___ / ___ / ___

_____

_____

_____

_____

WEDNESDAY ___ / ___ / ___

_____

_____

_____

_____

THURSDAY ___ / ___ / ___

_____

_____

_____

_____

_____

FRIDAY ___ / ___ / ___

_____

_____

_____

_____

SATURDAY ___ / ___ / ___

_____

_____

_____

_____

SUNDAY ___ / ___ / ___

_____

_____

_____

_____

_____

Your Twenty-Fifth Week

You always cry when _____
_____
_____.

MONDAY ___ / ___ / ___

_____
_____
_____
_____
_____

TUESDAY ___ / ___ / ___

_____

_____

_____

_____

WEDNESDAY ___ / ___ / ___

_____

_____

_____

_____

THURSDAY ___ / ___ / ___

_____

_____

_____

_____

_____

FRIDAY ___ / ___ / ___

_____

_____

_____

_____

SATURDAY ___ / ___ / ___

_____

_____

_____

_____

SUNDAY ___ / ___ / ___

_____

_____

_____

_____

_____

Your Twenty-Sixth Week

You made a puckered-up face when you first ate _____

_____

_____ .

MONDAY ____ / ____ / ____

_____

_____

_____

_____

_____

TUESDAY ___ / ___ / ___

_____

_____

_____

_____

WEDNESDAY ___ / ___ / ___

_____

_____

_____

_____

THURSDAY ___ / ___ / ___

_____

_____

_____

_____

_____

FRIDAY ___ / ___ / ___

_____

_____

_____

_____

SATURDAY ___ / ___ / ___

_____

_____

_____

_____

SUNDAY ___ / ___ / ___

_____

_____

_____

_____

_____

Your Twenty-Seventh Week

You are so fascinated by _____

_____

_____.

MONDAY ___ / ___ / ___

_____

_____

_____

_____

TUESDAY ___ / ___ / ___

_____

_____

_____

_____

WEDNESDAY ___ / ___ / ___

_____

_____

_____

_____

THURSDAY ___ / ___ / ___

_____

_____

_____

_____

_____

FRIDAY ___ / ___ / ___

_____

_____

_____

SATURDAY ___ / ___ / ___

_____

_____

_____

SUNDAY ___ / ___ / ___

_____

_____

_____

_____

Your Twenty-Eighth Week

Our most embarrassing moment together was when _____

_____

_____.

MONDAY ____ / ____ / ____

_____

_____

_____

_____

_____

TUESDAY ___ / ___ / ___

_____

_____

_____

_____

WEDNESDAY ___ / ___ / ___

_____

_____

_____

_____

THURSDAY ___ / ___ / ___

_____

_____

_____

_____

_____

FRIDAY ___ / ___ / ___

SATURDAY ___ / ___ / ___

SUNDAY ___ / ___ / ___

Your Twenty-Ninth Week

Your favorite thing to sleep with is _____

_____

_____.

MONDAY ____ / ____ / ____

_____

_____

_____

_____

_____

TUESDAY ___ / ___ / ___

_____

_____

_____

_____

WEDNESDAY ___ / ___ / ___

_____

_____

_____

_____

THURSDAY ___ / ___ / ___

_____

_____

_____

_____

_____

FRIDAY ___ / ___ / ___

_____

_____

_____

_____

SATURDAY ___ / ___ / ___

_____

_____

_____

_____

SUNDAY ___ / ___ / ___

_____

_____

_____

_____

Your Thirtieth Week

Your first imitated sound was _____

_____

_____.

MONDAY ___ / ___ / ___

_____

_____

_____

_____

_____

TUESDAY ___ / ___ / ___

_____

_____

_____

_____

WEDNESDAY ___ / ___ / ___

_____

_____

_____

_____

THURSDAY ___ / ___ / ___

_____

_____

_____

_____

FRIDAY ___ / ___ / ___

_____

_____

_____

_____

SATURDAY ___ / ___ / ___

_____

_____

_____

_____

SUNDAY ___ / ___ / ___

_____

_____

_____

_____

_____

Your Thirty-
First Week

Your first trip was to _____

_____

_____.

MONDAY ____ / ____ / ____

_____

_____

_____

_____

TUESDAY ___ / ___ / ___

_____

_____

_____

_____

WEDNESDAY ___ / ___ / ___

_____

_____

_____

_____

THURSDAY ___ / ___ / ___

_____

_____

_____

_____

_____

FRIDAY ___ / ___ / ___

_____

_____

_____

_____

SATURDAY ___ / ___ / ___

_____

_____

_____

_____

SUNDAY ___ / ___ / ___

_____

_____

_____

_____

_____

Your Thirty-Second Week

Some of my favorite nicknames for you are _____

_____

_____.

MONDAY ___ / ___ / ___

_____

_____

_____

_____

_____

TUESDAY ___ / ___ / ___

_____

_____

_____

_____

WEDNESDAY ___ / ___ / ___

_____

_____

_____

_____

THURSDAY ___ / ___ / ___

_____

_____

_____

_____

_____

FRIDAY ___ / ___ / ___

_____

_____

_____

_____

SATURDAY ___ / ___ / ___

_____

_____

_____

_____

SUNDAY ___ / ___ / ___

_____

_____

_____

_____

_____

Your Thirty-Third Week

The first time you saw a pet, you _____

_____

_____.

MONDAY ___ / ___ / ___

_____

_____

_____

_____

_____

TUESDAY ___ / ___ / ___

_____

_____

_____

_____

WEDNESDAY ___ / ___ / ___

_____

_____

_____

_____

THURSDAY ___ / ___ / ___

_____

_____

_____

_____

FRIDAY ___ / ___ / ___

_____

_____

_____

_____

SATURDAY ___ / ___ / ___

_____

_____

_____

_____

SUNDAY ___ / ___ / ___

_____

_____

_____

_____

_____

Your Thirty-Fourth Week

I hope you never forget that _____

_____

_____.

MONDAY ____ / ____ / ____

_____

_____

_____

_____

_____

TUESDAY ___ / ___ / ___

_____

_____

_____

_____

WEDNESDAY ___ / ___ / ___

_____

_____

_____

_____

THURSDAY ___ / ___ / ___

_____

_____

_____

_____

_____

FRIDAY ___ / ___ / ___

_____

_____

_____

_____

SATURDAY ___ / ___ / ___

_____

_____

_____

_____

SUNDAY ___ / ___ / ___

_____

_____

_____

_____

_____

Your Thirty-Fifth Week

Your reaction to discovering your hands and feet was _____

_____

_____ .

MONDAY ___ / ___ / ___

_____

_____

_____

_____

_____

TUESDAY ___ / ___ / ___

_____

_____

_____

_____

WEDNESDAY ___ / ___ / ___

_____

_____

_____

_____

THURSDAY ___ / ___ / ___

_____

_____

_____

_____

_____

FRIDAY ___ / ___ / ___

_____

_____

_____

_____

SATURDAY ___ / ___ / ___

_____

_____

_____

_____

SUNDAY ___ / ___ / ___

_____

_____

_____

_____

_____

Your Thirty-Sixth Week

The first thing that scared or frightened you was _____

_____

_____.

MONDAY ____ / ____ / ____

_____

_____

_____

_____

_____

TUESDAY ___ / ___ / ___

_____

_____

_____

_____

WEDNESDAY ___ / ___ / ___

_____

_____

_____

_____

THURSDAY ___ / ___ / ___

_____

_____

_____

_____

_____

FRIDAY ___ / ___ / ___

_____

_____

_____

_____

SATURDAY ___ / ___ / ___

_____

_____

_____

_____

SUNDAY ___ / ___ / ___

_____

_____

_____

_____

_____

Your Thirty-Seventh Week

When you saw yourself in the mirror for the first time, you

_____

_____.

MONDAY ___ / ___ / ___

_____

_____

_____

_____

TUESDAY ___ / ___ / ___

_____

_____

_____

_____

WEDNESDAY ___ / ___ / ___

_____

_____

_____

_____

THURSDAY ___ / ___ / ___

_____

_____

_____

_____

_____

FRIDAY ___ / ___ / ___

_____

_____

_____

SATURDAY ___ / ___ / ___

_____

_____

_____

SUNDAY ___ / ___ / ___

_____

_____

_____

_____

Your Thirty-Eighth Week

The first time you responded to your name was _____

_____

_____ .

MONDAY ___ / ___ / ___

_____

_____

_____

_____

_____

TUESDAY ___ / ___ / ___

_____

_____

_____

_____

WEDNESDAY ___ / ___ / ___

_____

_____

_____

_____

THURSDAY ___ / ___ / ___

_____

_____

_____

_____

FRIDAY ___ / ___ / ___

_____

_____

_____

_____

SATURDAY ___ / ___ / ___

_____

_____

_____

_____

SUNDAY ___ / ___ / ___

_____

_____

_____

_____

Your Thirty-Ninth Week

My hope for you is that you learn _____

_____

_____.

MONDAY ___ / ___ / ___

_____

_____

_____

_____

TUESDAY ___ / ___ / ___

_____

_____

_____

WEDNESDAY ___ / ___ / ___

_____

_____

_____

THURSDAY ___ / ___ / ___

_____

_____

_____

_____

FRIDAY ___ / ___ / ___

_____

_____

_____

_____

SATURDAY ___ / ___ / ___

_____

_____

_____

_____

SUNDAY ___ / ___ / ___

_____

_____

_____

_____

_____

Your Fortieth
Week

You're learning how to use your hands. The first object you
grasped was _____

_____.

MONDAY ____ / ____ / ____

_____

_____

_____

_____

TUESDAY ___ / ___ / ___

_____

_____

_____

_____

WEDNESDAY ___ / ___ / ___

_____

_____

_____

_____

THURSDAY ___ / ___ / ___

_____

_____

_____

_____

_____

FRIDAY ___ / ___ / ___

_____

_____

_____

_____

SATURDAY ___ / ___ / ___

_____

_____

_____

_____

SUNDAY ___ / ___ / ___

_____

_____

_____

_____

_____

Your Forty-
First Week

My dream for you is that you aren't afraid of/to _____

_____

_____.

MONDAY ___ / ___ / ___

_____

_____

_____

_____

TUESDAY ___ / ___ / ___

_____

_____

_____

_____

WEDNESDAY ___ / ___ / ___

_____

_____

_____

_____

THURSDAY ___ / ___ / ___

_____

_____

_____

_____

_____

FRIDAY ___ / ___ / ___

_____

_____

_____

_____

SATURDAY ___ / ___ / ___

_____

_____

_____

_____

SUNDAY ___ / ___ / ___

_____

_____

_____

_____

_____

Your Forty-
Second Week

Your favorite animal is a(n) _____

_____

_____.

MONDAY ___ / ___ / ___

_____

_____

_____

_____

_____

TUESDAY ___ / ___ / ___

_____

_____

_____

_____

WEDNESDAY ___ / ___ / ___

_____

_____

_____

_____

THURSDAY ___ / ___ / ___

_____

_____

_____

_____

_____

FRIDAY ___ / ___ / ___

_____

_____

_____

_____

SATURDAY ___ / ___ / ___

_____

_____

_____

_____

SUNDAY ___ / ___ / ___

_____

_____

_____

_____

_____

Your Forty-Third Week

I love giving you kisses. You kiss back by _____
_____
_____.

MONDAY ____ / ____ / ____

_____
_____
_____
_____
_____

TUESDAY ___ / ___ / ___

_____

_____

_____

_____

WEDNESDAY ___ / ___ / ___

_____

_____

_____

_____

THURSDAY ___ / ___ / ___

_____

_____

_____

_____

_____

FRIDAY ___ / ___ / ___

_____

_____

_____

_____

SATURDAY ___ / ___ / ___

_____

_____

_____

_____

SUNDAY ___ / ___ / ___

_____

_____

_____

_____

_____

Your Forty-Fourth Week

Love comes in many forms. I hope you love _____

_____

_____.

MONDAY ___ / ___ / ___

_____

_____

_____

_____

TUESDAY ___ / ___ / ___

_____
_____
_____
_____

WEDNESDAY ___ / ___ / ___

_____
_____
_____
_____

THURSDAY ___ / ___ / ___

_____
_____
_____
_____

FRIDAY ___ / ___ / ___

_____

_____

_____

_____

SATURDAY ___ / ___ / ___

_____

_____

_____

_____

SUNDAY ___ / ___ / ___

_____

_____

_____

_____

_____

Your Forty-Fifth Week

Your favorite part of the day happens to be _____
_____
_____.

MONDAY ___ / ___ / ___

_____
_____
_____
_____

TUESDAY ___ / ___ / ___

_____

_____

_____

_____

WEDNESDAY ___ / ___ / ___

_____

_____

_____

_____

THURSDAY ___ / ___ / ___

_____

_____

_____

_____

_____

FRIDAY ___ / ___ / ___

_____

_____

_____

_____

SATURDAY ___ / ___ / ___

_____

_____

_____

_____

SUNDAY ___ / ___ / ___

_____

_____

_____

_____

_____

Your Forty-Sixth Week

The person you're always happy to see is _____

_____

_____.

MONDAY ___ / ___ / ___

_____

_____

_____

_____

TUESDAY ___ / ___ / ___

_____

_____

_____

_____

WEDNESDAY ___ / ___ / ___

_____

_____

_____

_____

THURSDAY ___ / ___ / ___

_____

_____

_____

_____

FRIDAY ___ / ___ / ___

_____

_____

_____

_____

SATURDAY ___ / ___ / ___

_____

_____

_____

_____

SUNDAY ___ / ___ / ___

_____

_____

_____

_____

_____

Your Forty-Seventh Week

Friends are fun. You always like to play with _____
_____
_____.

MONDAY ___ / ___ / ___

_____
_____
_____
_____

TUESDAY ___ / ___ / ___

_____

_____

_____

_____

WEDNESDAY ___ / ___ / ___

_____

_____

_____

_____

THURSDAY ___ / ___ / ___

_____

_____

_____

_____

FRIDAY ___ / ___ / ___

_____

_____

_____

_____

SATURDAY ___ / ___ / ___

_____

_____

_____

_____

SUNDAY ___ / ___ / ___

_____

_____

_____

_____

_____

Your Forty-Eighth Week

I think of you whenever I see _____

_____

_____.

MONDAY ___ / ___ / ___

_____

_____

_____

_____

_____

TUESDAY ___ / ___ / ___

_____

_____

_____

_____

WEDNESDAY ___ / ___ / ___

_____

_____

_____

_____

THURSDAY ___ / ___ / ___

_____

_____

_____

_____

_____

FRIDAY ___ / ___ / ___

_____

_____

_____

_____

SATURDAY ___ / ___ / ___

_____

_____

_____

_____

SUNDAY ___ / ___ / ___

_____

_____

_____

_____

_____

Your Forty-Ninth Week

You're learning how to throw a fit. Your first temper tantrum

happened when _____

_____.

MONDAY ___ / ___ / ___

_____

_____

_____

_____

_____

TUESDAY ___ / ___ / ___

_____

_____

_____

_____

WEDNESDAY ___ / ___ / ___

_____

_____

_____

_____

THURSDAY ___ / ___ / ___

_____

_____

_____

_____

_____

FRIDAY ___ / ___ / ___

_____

_____

_____

SATURDAY ___ / ___ / ___

_____

_____

_____

SUNDAY ___ / ___ / ___

_____

_____

_____

_____

Your Fiftieth Week

Your favorite game to play is _____

_____

_____

_____

_____.

MONDAY ___ / ___ / ___

_____

_____

_____

_____

_____

TUESDAY ___ / ___ / ___

_____

_____

_____

_____

WEDNESDAY ___ / ___ / ___

_____

_____

_____

_____

THURSDAY ___ / ___ / ___

_____

_____

_____

_____

FRIDAY ___ / ___ / ___

_____

_____

_____

_____

SATURDAY ___ / ___ / ___

_____

_____

_____

SUNDAY ___ / ___ / ___

_____

_____

_____

_____

Your Fifty-First Week

The most magical moment of our first year was _____

_____

_____.

MONDAY ___ / ___ / ___

_____

_____

_____

_____

TUESDAY ___ / ___ / ___

_____

_____

_____

_____

WEDNESDAY ___ / ___ / ___

_____

_____

_____

_____

THURSDAY ___ / ___ / ___

_____

_____

_____

_____

_____

FRIDAY ___ / ___ / ___

_____

_____

_____

_____

SATURDAY ___ / ___ / ___

_____

_____

_____

_____

SUNDAY ___ / ___ / ___

_____

_____

_____

_____

_____

Your Fifty-
Second Week

When you get excited, you _____

_____

_____ .

MONDAY ____ / ____ / ____

_____

_____

_____

_____

_____

TUESDAY ___ / ___ / ___

_____

_____

_____

_____

WEDNESDAY ___ / ___ / ___

_____

_____

_____

_____

THURSDAY ___ / ___ / ___

_____

_____

_____

_____

_____

FRIDAY ___ / ___ / ___

_____

_____

_____

_____

SATURDAY ___ / ___ / ___

_____

_____

_____

_____

SUNDAY ___ / ___ / ___

_____

_____

_____

_____

_____

MONTH ONE:
Your Big Firsts

"When you hold your baby in your arms the first
time and you think of all the things you can say and
do to influence him, it's a tremendous responsibility.
What you do with him and for him can influence not
only him, but everyone he meets and not for a day
or a month or a year but for time and for eternity."

– ROSE KENNEDY

DATE ____ / ____ / ____

On this day, you _____

_____

_____

_____

DATE ____ / ____ / ____

On this day, you _____

_____

_____

_____

DATE ____ / ____ / ____

On this day, you _____

_____

_____

_____

DATE ____ / ____ / ____

On this day, you _____

_____

_____

_____

MONTH TWO:
Your Big Firsts

"All things great are wound up with all things little."

– L. M. MONTGOMERY, *ANNE OF GREEN GABLES*

DATE ____ / ____ / ____

On this day, you _____

_____

_____

_____

DATE ___ / ___ / ___

On this day, you _____

_____

_____

_____

DATE ___ / ___ / ___

On this day, you _____

_____

_____

_____

_____

DATE ___ / ___ / ___

On this day, you _____

_____

_____

_____

_____

MONTH THREE:
Your Big Firsts

"We never know the love of a parent till we become
parents ourselves."

— HENRY WARD BEECHER

DATE ___ / ___ / ___

On this day, you _____

_____

_____

_____

DATE ___ / ___ / ___

On this day, you _____

_____

_____

_____

DATE ___ / ___ / ___

On this day, you _____

_____

_____

_____

DATE ___ / ___ / ___

On this day, you _____

_____

_____

_____

MONTH FOUR:
Your Big Firsts

"Love is our true destiny. We do not find
the meaning of life by ourselves alone—we
find it with another."

– THOMAS MERTON

DATE ____ / ____ / ____

On this day, you _____

_____

_____

_____

DATE ____ / ____ / ____

On this day, you _____

_____

_____

_____

DATE ____ / ____ / ____

On this day, you _____

_____

_____

_____

DATE ____ / ____ / ____

On this day, you _____

_____

_____

_____

MONTH FIVE:
Your Big Firsts

"To me there is no picture so beautiful as smiling,
bright-eyed, happy children; no music so sweet as
their clear and ringing laughter."

— P. T. BARNUM

DATE ____ / ____ / ____

On this day, you _____

_____

_____

_____

168

DATE ___ / ___ / ___

On this day, you _____

_____

_____

_____

DATE ___ / ___ / ___

On this day, you _____

_____

_____

_____

DATE ___ / ___ / ___

On this day, you _____

_____

_____

_____

MONTH SIX:
Your Big Firsts

"Oh, 'tis love, 'tis love, that makes the
world go round."

– LEWIS CARROLL, *ALICE'S ADVENTURES IN WONDERLAND*

DATE ___ / ___ / ___

On this day, you _____

_____

_____

_____

DATE ___ / ___ / ___

On this day, you _____

_____

_____

_____

DATE ___ / ___ / ___

On this day, you _____

_____

_____

_____

DATE ___ / ___ / ___

On this day, you _____

_____

_____

_____

MONTH SEVEN:
Your Big Firsts

"A heart is not judged by how much you love, but by how much you are loved by others."

– L. FRANK BAUM, *THE WONDERFUL WIZARD OF OZ*

DATE ___ / ___ / ___

On this day, you _____

_____

_____

_____

DATE ___ / ___ / ___

On this day, you _____

_____

_____

_____

DATE ___ / ___ / ___

On this day, you _____

_____

_____

_____

DATE ___ / ___ / ___

On this day, you _____

_____

_____

_____

MONTH EIGHT:
Your Big Firsts

"Even though you want to try to, never grow up."

– J. M. BARRIE, AUTHOR OF *PETER PAN*

DATE ___ / ___ / ___

On this day, you _____

_____

_____

_____

DATE ___ / ___ / ___

On this day, you _____

_____

_____

_____

DATE ___ / ___ / ___

On this day, you _____

_____

_____

_____

_____

DATE ___ / ___ / ___

On this day, you _____

_____

_____

_____

_____

MONTH NINE:
Your Big Firsts

"The best way to make children good is to
make them happy."

— OSCAR WILDE

DATE ____ / ____ / ____

On this day, you _____

_____

_____

_____

DATE ___ / ___ / ___

On this day, you _____

_____

_____

_____

DATE ___ / ___ / ___

On this day, you _____

_____

_____

_____

DATE ___ / ___ / ___

On this day, you _____

_____

_____

_____

MONTH TEN:
Your Big Firsts

"Children are not only innocent and curious
but also optimistic and joyful and
essentially happy. They are, in short,
everything adults wish they could be."

– CAROLYN HAYWOOD

DATE ____ / ____ / ____

On this day, you _____

_____

_____

_____

DATE ___ / ___ / ___

On this day, you _____

_____

_____

_____

DATE ___ / ___ / ___

On this day, you _____

_____

_____

_____

DATE ___ / ___ / ___

On this day, you _____

_____

_____

_____

MONTH ELEVEN:
Your Big Firsts

"Hugs can do great amounts of good—especially for children."

— PRINCESS DIANA

DATE ___ / ___ / ___

On this day, you _____

_____

_____

_____

DATE ___ / ___ / ___

On this day, you _____

_____

_____

_____

DATE ___ / ___ / ___

On this day, you _____

_____

_____

_____

_____

DATE ___ / ___ / ___

On this day, you _____

_____

_____

_____

_____

MONTH TWELVE:

Your Big Firsts

"Childhood is a short season."

— HELEN HAYES

DATE ____ / ____ / ____

On this day, you _____

_____

_____

_____

DATE ___ / ___ / ___

On this day, you _____

_____

_____

_____

DATE ___ / ___ / ___

On this day, you _____

_____

_____

_____

_____

DATE ___ / ___ / ___

On this day, you _____

_____

_____

_____

_____

"There are only two lasting bequests we can hope to give our children. One of these is roots, the other, wings."

— HODDING CARTER

The Little Details

You'll notice many changes in your little one throughout the first year. They'll transform from a tiny, helpless infant to an extremely active toddler at such a surprising rate that it may be hard for you to remember each stage of growth. The little details may not seem all that important now, as most of your time is spent changing diapers and admiring your new addition to the family. One day though, you'll look back and want to remember each stage—especially when your once-tiny baby stands taller than you. The little details now will be big memories later.

Grow, Baby, Grow!

Use this chart to record the month-by-month changes you observe and anything else you don't want to forget about your first year together.

MONTH	HEIGHT	WEIGHT	
Birth			
Coming Home			
One Month			
Two Months			
Three Months			
Four Months			
Five Months			
Six Months			
Seven Months			
Eight Months			
Nine Months			
Ten Months			
Eleven Months			
Baby's First Birthday!			

NOTES

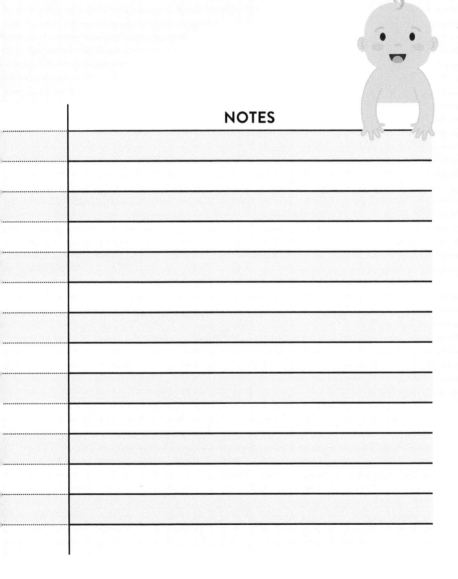

Baby, It's Time to Eat!

Use this chart to record your little one's food likes and dislikes.

You stopped night feeding at _____ weeks.

Your first solid food was _____

on _____ / _____ / _____ .

YOU LOVE...	YOU HATE...

Baby's Immunization Tracker

Baby's first year will be filled with what may seem like endless doctor appointments. During these appointments, your baby's doctor will check baby's growth and complete any routine preventive care. Use this section to record baby's immunizations. Check with your baby's doctor regarding the recommended schedule. For your convenience, this tracker continues beyond first-year immunizations so you can keep all immunization information together. You can also ask your baby's doctor for an immunization record card.

IMMUNIZATION	DATE	
Hepatitis B (HepB)		
Hepatitis B (HepB)		
Hepatitis B (HepB)		
Rotavirus (RV)		
Rotavirus (RV)		
Rotavirus (RV)		
Diphtheria, tetanus, pertussis (DTaP)		
Diphtheria, tetanus, pertussis (DTaP)		
Diphtheria, tetanus, pertussis (DTaP)		
Diphtheria, tetanus, pertussis (DTaP)		
Diphtheria, tetanus, pertussis (DTaP)		
Haemophilus influenzae type b (Hib)		
Haemophilus influenzae type b (Hib)		
Haemophilus influenzae type b (Hib)		
Haemophilus influenzae type b (Hib)		
Pneumococcal (PCV)		
Pneumococcal (PCV)		

NOTES

Continued . . .

Continued from previous page.

IMMUNIZATION	DATE	
Pneumococcal (PCV)		
Pneumococcal (PCV)		
Polio (IPV)		
Polio (IPV)		
Polio (IPV)		
Polio (IPV)		
Measles, mumps, rubella (MMR)		
Measles, mumps, rubella (MMR)		
Varicella		
Varicella		
Hepatitis A (HepA)		
Hepatitis A (HepA)		
Influenza (yearly)		
Influenza (yearly)		
Influenza (yearly)		
Influenza (yearly)		
Influenza (yearly)		

NOTES

Baby's First Celebrations and Holidays

Baby's first year will be full of new and exciting adventures. Use this section to capture those memories. Write down all the memorable events, special occasions, and holidays you and baby experienced together. Some examples may include their first visit to the park or memories from their first birthday.

YOUR FIRST

....

DATE ___ / ___ / ___

The celebration was: _____

_____

_____

These people came: _____

_____

_____

_____

The thing you loved the most was: _____

_____

_____

_____

YOUR FIRST

....

DATE ___ / ___ / ___

The celebration was: _____

_____

_____

These people came: _____

_____

_____

_____

The thing you loved the most was: _____

_____

_____

_____

YOUR FIRST

....

DATE ___ / ___ / ___

The celebration was: _____

_____

_____

These people came: _____

_____

_____

_____

The thing you loved the most was: _____

_____

_____

_____

YOUR FIRST

....

DATE ____ / ____ / ____

The celebration was: _____

_____

_____

These people came: _____

_____

_____

_____

The thing you loved the most was: _____

_____

_____

_____

YOUR FIRST

....

DATE ___ / ___ / ___

The celebration was: _____

_____

_____

These people came: _____

_____

_____

_____

The thing you loved the most was: _____

_____

_____

_____

YOUR FIRST

....

DATE ____ / ____ / ____

The celebration was: _____

_____

_____

These people came: _____

_____

_____

_____

The thing you loved the most was: _____

_____

_____

_____

YOUR FIRST

....

DATE ____ / ____ / ____

The celebration was: _____

_____

_____

These people came: _____

_____

_____

_____

The thing you loved the most was: _____

_____

_____

_____

YOUR FIRST

....

DATE ____ / ____ / ____

The celebration was: _____

_____

_____

These people came: _____

_____

_____

_____

The thing you loved the most was: _____

_____

_____

_____

YOUR FIRST

....

DATE ____ / ____ / ____

The celebration was: _____

_____

_____

These people came: _____

_____

_____

_____

The thing you loved the most was: _____

_____

_____

_____

YOUR FIRST

....

DATE ____ / ____ / ____

The celebration was: _____

_____

_____

These people came: _____

_____

_____

_____

The thing you loved the most was: _____

_____

_____

_____

A Letter to You, Baby

Congratulations! You made it. You've finished your first year of parenting—you deserve an award. This is a special place for you to reflect back on your first year with baby, and to express your hopes and dreams for baby's future. Use the previous pages to spark some memories and inspiration! Then write your little one a letter to have and keep forever.

_____

_____

_____

_____

_____

_____

_____

_____

_____

_____

_____

_____